G. SCHIRMER'S
COLLECTION OF
OPERA LIBRETTOS

DER
FLIEGENDE HOLLÄNDER

Opera in Three Acts

by

Richard Wagner

English Version by
STEWART ROBB

Ed. 2584

G. SCHIRMER, *Inc.*

45675c

THE FLYING DUTCHMAN

The Flying Dutchman is the first of Richard Wagner's thirteen operas in which his essential musical individuality emerges. Its predecessor, *Rienzi,* for years the composer's only successful work, is a grandiose epic written in the French grand opera style of Meyerbeer and Spontini. Though *The Flying Dutchman* places no emphasis on ornate spectacle, it does retain many conventions of old-fashioned opera: set arias, duets, trios and ensembles. The music, however, points to Wagner's later style in that for the first time he makes use of the *Leitmotiv* technique, later greatly developed. Furthermore, the basic plot is one that Wagner was to utilize in his next two operas, *Tannhäuser* and *Lohengrin*: the search of a proud, lonely man for the redeeming, unquestioning love of a woman. Wagner doubtless identified himself closely with this search.

The folk legend of a sea captain doomed to sail the seven seas for eternity is ageless. Wagner adapted his libretto from a play by Heinrich Heine, who in turn had taken his drama from an English stage work by one Fitzball. First-hand inspiration for his score came to Wagner during a rough ocean journey from Riga to Paris, where he was going in the hope of bettering his fortunes. During the stormy passage, the sound of hollow wind and the sting of salt spray seem to have been deeply impressed on Wagner's musical mind. In Paris, where he completed his opera in 1841, the composer was forced to take all manner of odd jobs to survive: proofreading, arranging and writing songs. At one point he even had to sell the libretto of *The Flying Dutchman* to another composer to raise cash.

His own setting of the text did not reach the stage until January 2, 1843, at Dresden, where his *Rienzi* had scored a popular hit. The new work, presented in a single act, was given a poor performance and withdrawn from the repertory after four performances. Another production in Berlin met a similar fate. Only with the establishment of Wagner's other works, which still tend to overshadow *The Flying Dutchman,* did the opera find a lasting place in the standard repertory. It was the first Wagner opera given in England (1873), sung in Italian at Queen Victoria's request. It first came to the United States on November 8, 1876, at the Philadelphia Academy of Music, again in Italian. New York first heard *The Flying Dutchman* in English, in 1877. The work finally dropped anchor at the Metropolitan Opera House on opening night of the 1889-90 season, when it was conducted by Anton Seidl; the cast included Theodor Reichman in the title role, Sophie Weisner as Senta and Emil Fischer as Daland.

Today it is no longer possible to hear in *The Flying Dutchman* those many musical novelties that puzzled and shocked Wagner's contemporaries. Still, in the light of his later output and in the light of the operas of Weber and Beethoven, the work can safely be called his first true music drama.

THE STORY

ACT I. A violent storm has driven Daland's ship several miles beyond his home on the Norwegian coast. After telling his crew that they have earned a good rest, he leaves the watch in charge of a young steersman, who falls asleep singing a ballad about his sweetheart. As the sky suddenly darkens and the waters again grow rough, a ghostly red-sailed schooner appears on the horizon and drops anchor next to Daland's ship. Its captain, Vanderdecken, steps ashore, despairing of his fate: once every seven years he may leave his ship in search of a woman whose perfect love will redeem him from his deathless wandering; failing this, he is condemned to roam until the Day of Judgment. When Daland returns to discover the phantom ship, Vanderdecken tells him of his plight and offers a reward of gold and jewels for a night's lodging. Then, discovering that Daland has a daughter, the Dutchman asks for her hand in marriage. Daland, seeing the extent of the stranger's wealth, immediately agrees and rejoices in his good fortune. Vanderdecken promises his entire treasure cargo as dowry and renews hope for his salvation. The happy Daland, agreeing to meet the Dutchman at his home port, sets sail with his crew, who take up the steersman's song.

ACT II. Daland's young daughter Senta dreamily watches a group of her friends who sit spinning in the family living room under the watchful eye of Mary, her nurse. The girls tease Senta about her suitor, the huntsman Erik, but she remains almost in a trance, staring at a portrait of the Flying Dutchman on the wall. When the superstitious Mary refuses to sing a ballad about the phantom captain, Senta begins the song with burning intensity; to the dismay of her friends, she prays that she may be the one to save the lost man. Erik enters with news of the sailors' return; Mary and the others rush out to prepare the homecoming feast. The huntsman remains behind and asks the reluctant Senta to plead his cause with Daland. Noticing her preoccupation with the Dutchman's picture, he relates a frightening dream in which he saw her passionately embrace the Dutchman and sail away on his ship. Senta, however, does not hide her true feelings from Erik, who leaves in despair. A moment later, Vanderdecken steps before the girl, who stands transfixed. Daland quickly follows and bids his daughter welcome the stranger, whom he has brought to be her husband. After he leaves, the Dutchman tells of his sad lot, testing Senta's compassion and trust; she ecstatically vows to be faithful to him unto death. Daland comes back and is overjoyed to learn that his daughter has consented to be Vanderdecken's bride.

ACT III. At the harbor, the villagers celebrate the sailors' return with singing and dancing. Perplexed by the strange silence aboard the Dutchman's ship, they invite his men to share the festivities and toast the neighboring vessel. In answer to the greeting, the ghostly crew deride their captain's quest in hollow chanting; the villagers run away in terror. Senta soon rushes in, pursued by Erik, who insists that she has pledged him her love. Vanderdecken overhears the huntsman's claim and brands Senta a faithless woman, bidding his salvation farewell. Senta pleads with him to hear her out, but the Dutchman replies that since she has not yet proclaimed her vows before God, she will escape the eternal damnation of those who betray him. As she replies that she knows his identity and means to save him from his fate, Vanderdecken leaps aboard his vessel just as it sets sail, revealing that he is the Flying Dutchman. While Erik, Mary and Daland stand transfixed in horror, Senta, triumphantly crying that she is faithful unto death, runs to the edge of the fjord and throws herself into the raging sea. Vanderdecken's ship is seen sinking on the horizon as the transfigured Senta and Flying Dutchman rise to heaven.

Courtesy Opera News

CAST OF CHARACTERS

DALAND, a Norwegian sea captain . . . . Bass

SENTA, his daughter . . . . Soprano

ERIK, a huntsman . . . . Tenor

MARY, Senta's nurse . . . . Contralto

STEERSMAN of Daland's ship . . . . Tenor

THE DUTCHMAN . . . . Baritone

Sailors and villagers

SYNOPSIS OF SCENES

DER FLIEGENDE HOLLÄNDER

ERSTER AUFZUG

Steiles Felsenufer

Das Meer nimmt den grössten Teil der Bühne ein; weite Aussicht auf dasselbe. Finsteres Wetter; heftiger Sturm. Das Schiff Dalands hat soeben dicht am Ufer Anker geworfen; die Matrosen sind in geräuschvoller Arbeit beschäftigt, die Segel aufzuhissen, Taue auszuwerfen usw. Daland ist an das Land gegangen; er ersteigt einen Felsen und sieht landeinwärts, die Gegend zu erkennen.

MATROSEN

(während der Arbeit)

Hojoje! Hojoje! Hallojo! Ho!

DALAND

(vom Felsen herabkommend)

Kein Zweifel! Sieben Meilen fort
trieb uns der Sturm vom sich'ren Port.
So nah' dem Ziel nach langer Fahrt
war mir der Streich noch aufgespart!

STEUERMANN

(von Bord rufend)

Ho! Kapitän!

DALAND

An Bord bei euch, wie steht's?

STEUERMANN

Gut, Kapitän! Wir haben sich'ren
Grund!

DALAND

Sandwike ist's! Genau kenn' ich die
Bucht.
Verwünscht! Schon sah am Ufer ich
mein Haus!
Senta, mein Kind, glaubt' ich schon zu
umarmen!
Da bläst es aus dem Teufelsloch
heraus . . .
Wer baut auf Wind, baut auf Satans
Erbarmen!

(an Bord gehend)

Was hilft's! Geduld, der Sturm lässt
nach;
wenn er so tobt währt's nicht lang.
He, Bursche! Lange war't ihr wach:
Zur Ruhe denn! Mir ist nicht bang!

*(Die Matrosen steigen in den
Schiffsraum hinab.)*

Nun, Steuermann, die Wache nimmst
du wohl für mich?
Gefahr ist nicht, doch gut ist's, wenn
du wachst.

STEUERMANN

Seid ausser Sorg'! Schlaft ruhig,
Kapitän!

(Daland geht in die Kajüte. Der Steuermann allein auf dem Verdeck. Der Sturm hat sich etwas gelegt und wiederholt sich nur in abgesetzten Pausen; in hoher See türmen sich die Wellen. Der Steuermann macht noch einmal die Runde, dann setzt er sich am Ruder nieder.)

STEUERMANN

Mit Gewitter und Sturm aus fernem
Meer—
mein Mädel, bin ich dir nah!
Über turmhohe Flut vom Süden her—
mein Mädel, ich bin da!
Mein Mädel, wenn nicht Südwind wär',
ich nimmer wohl käm' zu dir:
Ach, lieber Südwind blas noch mehr!
Mein Mädel verlangt nach mir.
Hohoje! Halloho! Jolohohoho!

(Eine Woge schwillt an und rüttelt heftig das Schiff. Der Steuermann fährt auf und sieht nach; er überzeugt sich, dass kein Schade geschehen, setzt sich wieder und singt, während ihn die Schläfrigkeit immer mehr übermannt.)

Von des Südens Gestad's, aus weitem
Land—
ich hab' an dich gedacht;
durch Gewitter und Meer vom Mohrenstrand—
hab' dir 'was mitgebracht.
Mein Mädel, preis' den Südwind hoch,
ich bring' dir ein gülden Band:
Ach, lieber Südwind, blase doch!
Mein Mädel hätt' gern den Tand.
Hohoje! Halloho!

(Er kämpft mit der Müdigkeit und schläft endlich ein. Der Sturm beginnt von neuem heftig zu wüten; es wird finsterer. In der Ferne zeigt sich das Schiff des "Fliegenden Holländers" mit blutroten Segeln und schwarzen Masten. Es naht sich schnell der Küste nach der, dem Schiffe des Norwegers entgegengesetzten, Seite; mit einem furchtbaren Krach sinkt der Anker in den Grund. — Der Steuermann zuckt aus dem Schlafe auf; ohne seine Stellung zu verlassen, blickt er flüchtig nach dem Steuer, und, überzeugt, dass kein

THE FLYING DUTCHMAN

ACT ONE

A steep, rocky shore. The sea occupies the greater part of the scene, and there is a wide view over it. Gloomy weather. A violent storm.

(Daland's ship has just cast anchor close to the shore; the sailors are noisily employed in furling the sails, coiling ropes, etc. Daland has gone on shore. He climbs upon a rock and surveys the country to find out where they are.)

CHORUS OF SAILORS
(at work)

Hoyohey! Halloyo! Hoyohey! Ho!

DALAND
(coming down from the rock)

I knew it! This the storm has done!
We're thirty miles and more from port.
And just when we were near our goal!
Blows such as this are hard to take!

STEERSMAN
(calling from deck)

Ho! Captain!

DALAND

You there on board, what cheer?

STEERSMAN

Good! All is well! The anch'rage here is safe.

DALAND

Sandwyke strand, I know this bay quite well.
Be damned! Just as I saw my house on shore,
Just as I fancied I kissed my daughter Senta,
There came a blast that blew from hell itself!
Who trusts the wind, trusts in Satan's compassion! *(going on board)*
Why talk? Just wait. The storm will pass.
Such raging frenzy does not last.
Hey, hearties, you have kept long watch;
So take a rest, all now goes well!
(Sailors go below.)

Say, steersman, would you mind keeping watch for me?
The danger's past, it's good though that you watch.

STEERSMAN

Depend on me! Sleep calmly! All is well!

(Daland goes down into the cabin. The steersman is alone on deck. The storm has somewhat subsided and returns only at intervals; out at sea the waves are tossing high. The steersman walks round the deck once and then sits down near the wheel.)

STEERSMAN

Through the lightning and storm from seas afar,
My sweetheart, I am near!
Over towering waves by southwind urged,
My sweetheart, I am here!
My sweetheart, if no southwind blew,
I'd never have come to you.
Ah, good man southwind, blow some more!
My sweetheart, she loves me true!
Hohoyo! Hallohoho, yolloho, ho, ho!

(A wave strikes and shakes the ship violently. The steersman starts up and looks about him. Satisfied that no harm has been done, he sits down again and sings while drowsiness gradually overpowers him.)

On the shores of the south, in distant land,
I have you in my thoughts;
Through the lightning and sea, from Moorish strand,
Accept the gift I've brought.
My sweetheart, praise the southwind well,
I bring you a golden chain;
Ah, trusty southwind, blow some more!
These trinkets she won't disdain!
Hohoyeh! hollaho!

(He struggles against fatigue, and at last falls asleep. The storm again begins to rage violently, and it grows darker. In the distance appears the

1

Schade geschehen, brummt er den Anfang seines Liedes "Mein Mädel, wenn nicht Südwind wär" und schläft von neuem ein.—Stumm und ohne das geringste Geräusch hisst die gespenstische Mannschaft des Holländers die Segel auf. Der Holländer kommt an das Land.)

HOLLÄNDER

Die Frist ist um, und abermals verstrichen
sind sieben Jahr'. Voll Überdruss wirft mich
das Meer ans Land . . . Ha, stolzer Ozean!
In kurzer Frist sollst du mich wieder tragen!
Dein Trotz ist beugsam—doch ewig meine Qual!
Das Heil, das auf dem Land ich suche, nie werd' ich es finden! Euch, des Weltmeers Fluten, bleib' ich getreu, bis eure letzte Welle sich bricht, und euer letztes Nass versiegt!
Wie oft in Meeres tiefsten Schlund stürzt' ich voll Sehnsucht mich hinab:
Doch ach! den Tod, ich fand ihn nicht!
Da, wo der Schiffe furchtbar Grab, trieb *mein* Schiff ich zum Klippengrund:
Doch ach! mein Grab, es schloss sich nicht!
Verhöhnend droht' ich dem Piraten, im wilden Kampfe hofft' ich Tod;
"Hier"—rief ich—„zeige dein Taten!
Von Schätzen voll ist Schiff und Boot."
Doch ach! des Meer's barbar'scher Sohn
schlägt bang' das Kreuz und flieht davon.
Wie oft in Meeres tiefsten Schlund stürzt' ich voll Sehnsucht mich hinab:
Doch ach! den Tod, ich fand ihn nicht!
Da, wo der Schiffe furchtbar Grab, trieb *mein* Schiff ich zum Klippengrund:
Nirgends ein Grab! Niemals der Tod!
Dies der Verdammnis Schreckgebot.
Dich frage ich, gepriesner Engel Gottes, der meines Heils Bedingung mir gewann:
War ich Unsel'ger Spielwerk deines Spottes,
als die Erlösung du mir zeigtest an?
Vergebne Hoffnung! Furchtbar eitler Wahn!
Um ew'ge Treu' auf Erden—ist's getan!

Nur *eine* Hoffnung soll mir bleiben,
nur *eine* unerschüttert stehn:
so lang der Erde Keime treiben,
so muss sie doch zugrunde gehn.
Tag des Gerichtes! Jüngster Tag!
Wann brichst du an in meine Nacht?
Wann dröhnt er, der Vernichtungsschlag,
mit dem die Welt zusammenkracht?
Wann alle Toten auferstehn,
dann werde ich in Nichts vergehn.
Ihr Welten, endet euren Lauf!
Ew'ge Vernichtung, nimm mich auf!

MANNSCHAFT DES HOLLÄNDERS
(aus dem Schiffsraum)
Ew'ge Vernichtung, nimm uns auf!
(Daland erscheint auf dem Verdeck seines Schiffes; er sieht sich nach dem Winde um, erblickt das Schiff des Holländers und wendet sich zum Steuermann.)

DALAND
He! Holla! Steuermann!

STEUERMANN
(sich schlaftrunken halb aufrichtend)
'S ist nichts! 'S ist nichts!
Ach, lieber Südwind, blas noch mehr, mein Mädel . . .

DALAND
(ihn heftig aufrüttelnd)
Du siehst nichts? Gelt, du wachest brav, mein Bursch!
Dort liegt ein Schiff . . . wie lange schliefst du schon?

STEUERMANN
(rasch auffahrend)
Zum Teufel auch! Verzeiht mir, Kapitän!
(Er setzt hastig das Sprachrohr an und ruft der Mannschaft des Holländers zu.)
Wer da? *(Pause, keine Antwort)*
Wer da? *(Pause)*

DALAND
Es scheint, sie sind gerad' so faul als wir.

STEUERMANN
(wie vorher)
Gebt Antwort! Schiff und Flagge?

DALAND
(indem er den Holländer am Lande erblickt)
Lass ab! Mich dünkt, ich seh' den Kapitän.
He! Holla! Seemann! Nenne dich!
Wess' Landes?

ship of the Flying Dutchman, with blood-red sails and black masts. She quickly nears the shore, over against the ship of the Norwegian. With fearful crash the anchor plunges into the water. The steersman springs up out of sleep; without leaving his place he gives a hasty look at the wheel, and, satisfied that no harm has been done, he hums the beginning of his song: "My sweetheart, if no southwind blew." He sleeps again. Silently, and without the least further noise, the spectral crew of the Dutchman furl the sails, etc. The Dutchman goes on shore.)

THE DUTCHMAN

The term is up, and once again are
    ended
My seven years. The sated sea has cast
    me
On the land . . . Ha, haughty ocean!
A little while and you again will bear
    me!
Your spite is fitful, my torment has
    no end!
The cure, which on the land I seek
    for, never
Shall I find it! You, O world-wide
    ocean,
Will find me true, until your final
    billow
Shall roll, until at last you dry away!
How many times I've longed to die,
Hurling myself into the deep,
But death, alas, I never found!
There, where the ships find grisly
    graves
I've plunged into the rocky reefs,
But ah, my grave, it opened not!
With scorn I gave threats to the
    pirate,
And hoped for death in savage fray.
"Here," cried I, "let me see your
    mettle!
I've treasures here in ship and boat!"
But ah! the sea's barbaric son
Just hoisted cross and fled in fear!
Nowhere a grave! Never to die!
This is damnation's horrid curse!
Then do I ask, sweet angel sent from
    heaven,
Who won for me the blessed hope of
    grace,
Was I the wretched plaything of your
    mock'ry
When I was shown the way to save
    myself?

Oh, hope most empty! Fearful, idle
    dream!
Eternal truth no longer lives on earth!
There's just one hope I still can
    harbor,
Just one alone that stands secure:
Though earthly seed may last for
    eons,
It still must one day have an end.
Great day of Judgment, final day!
When will you dawn upon my night?
I wait you, pulverizing blow,
To crack the world and bring its doom!
When all the dead are raised again,
Then nothingness will end my pain!
You planets, cease to whirl about,
Endless oblivion, blot me out!

CHORUS OF SAILORS

Endless oblivion, blot us out!

(Daland comes out of the cabin; he looks around at the storm, and observes the strange ship. He sees the steersman.)

DALAND

Hey! Holla! Steersman!

STEERSMAN

(half-roused from sleep)

All's well, all's well.
Ah! kindly southwind, blow some more,
My sweetheart—

DALAND

(shaking him violently)

Can't you see? Say, fine watch you
keep, my lad! There lies a ship! How
long were you asleep?

STEERSMAN

(starting up)

Well I'll be damned! Excuse me for
this, sir! *(He calls through the
speaking trumpet.)* Ahoy! Ahoy!
(The sound echoes each time.)

DALAND

It seems that they are lazy men, like
us.

STEERSMAN

Give answer! Ship and colors!

DALAND

(perceiving the Dutchman on the land)

Forbear! I think I see the captain
there! Hey! Holla! Seaman! What's
your name—your country?

(a long silence)

HOLLÄNDER
(*nach einer Pause, ohne seine Stellung zu verlassen*)
Weit komm ich her: Verwehrt bei Sturm und Wetter
ihr mir den Ankerplatz?

DALAND
Verhüt es Gott!
Gastfreundschaft kennt der Seemann.
(*an Land gehend*)
Wer bist du?

HOLLÄNDER
Holländer.

DALAND
Gott zum Gruss! So trieb auch dich
der Sturm an diesen nackten Felsenstrand?
Mir ging's nicht besser; wenig Meilen nur
von hier ist meine Heimat, fast erreicht,
musst' ich aufs neu' mich von ihr wenden. Sag,
woher kommst du? Hast Schaden du genommen?

HOLLÄNDER
Mein Schiff ist fest, es leidet keinen Schaden.
Durch Sturm und bösen Wind verschlagen,
irr' auf den Wassern ich umher —
wie lange, weiss ich kaum zu sagen:
schon zähl' ich nicht die Jahre mehr.
Unmöglich dünkt mich's, dass ich nenne
die Länder alle, die ich fand:
das eine nur, nach dem ich brenne,
ich find es nicht, mein Heimatland!
Vergönne mir auf kurze Frist dein Haus,
und deine Freundschaft soll dich nicht gereun.
Mit Schätzen aller Gegenden und Zonen
ist reich mein Schiff beladen, willst du handeln,
so sollst du sicher deines Vorteils sein.

DALAND
Wie wunderbar! Soll deinem Wort ich glauben?
Ein Unstern, scheint's, hat dich bis jetzt verfolgt.
Um dir zu frommen, biet' ich, was ich kann:
Doch—darf ich fragen, was dein Schiff enthält?

HOLLÄNDER
(*gibt seiner Mannschaft ein Zeichen, zwei von derselben bringen eine Kiste ans Land.*)

Die seltensten der Schätze sollst du sehn,
kostbare Perlen, edelstes Gestein
Blick hin und überzeuge dich vom Werte
des Preises, den ich für ein gastlich' Dach
dir biete!

DALAND
(*voll Erstaunen den Inhalt der Kiste prüfend*)
Wie? Ist's möglich? Diese Schätze!
Wer ist so reich, den Preis dafür zu bieten?

HOLLÄNDER
Den Preis? Soeben hab' ich ihn genannt:
Dies für das Obdach einer einz'gen Nacht!
Doch, was du siehst, ist nur der kleinste Teil
von dem, was meines Schiffes Raum verschliesst.
Was frommt der Schatz? Ich habe' weder Weib
noch Kind, und meine Heimat find' ich nie!
All meinen Reichtum biet' ich dir, wenn bei
den Deinen du mir neue Heimat gibst.

DALAND
Was muss ich hören!

HOLLÄNDER
Hast du eine Tochter?

DALAND
Fürwahr, ein treues Kind.

HOLLÄNDER
Sie sei mein Weib!

DALAND
(*freudig betroffen*)
Wie? Hör' ich recht? Meine Tochter sei sein Weib?
Er selbst spricht aus den Gedanken . . .
Fast fürcht' ich, wenn unentschlossen ich bleib',
er müsst' im Vorsatze wanken.
Wüsst ich, ob ich wach' oder träume!
Kann ein Eidam willkommener sein?
Ein Tor, wenn das Glück ich versäume!
Voll Entzücken schlage ich ein.

HOLLÄNDER
Ach, ohne Weib, ohne Kind bin ich,
nichts fesselt mich an die Erde!

THE DUTCHMAN

(*without leaving his place*)

Far from this place. Do not refuse me
anchorage during this stormy time.

DALAND

The Lord forbid! Kind welcome comes
from seamen!

(*going on shore*)

Who are you?

THE DUTCHMAN

Hollander.

DALAND

God be with you! Has tempest
forced you too upon this barren,
rocky shore?
I fared no better. I was sailing
To my home a few miles distant;
almost there,
I had to turn again and leave it.
Say, from where are you? Have you
had any damage?

THE DUTCHMAN

My ship is tight; it has not suffered
damage.
The driving wind and hostile tempest
Force me to wander through the
waves.
How long though? Hardly can I tell
you:
Long have I ceased to count the years.
Indeed, I doubt if I could give you
The names of all the lands I found.
The only one I truly long for,
I find it not—my native land!
Oh let me stay within your home a
while:
You'll not repent such friendship shown
to me.
My ship is richly laden with fine
treasures
From every clime and country. Will
you traffic?
For if you do your profit will be sure.

DALAND

How wonderful! Can I believe your
story?
A star of ill has followed you till now.
I'll try to help you in what way I can.
Yet dare I ask you what your ship
contains?

THE DUTCHMAN

(*making a sign to the watch on his
ship, where upon they bring a chest
to shore*)

The rarest of all treasures shall you see.
Pearls that are priceless, stones of
untold wealth.
Look in, discover for yourself the
worth
Of the treasures offered here for just
a friendly hearthside.

DALAND

(*looking at the contents of the chest
with wonder*)

What!
Fantastic! All these treasures!
Who is so rich to make an equal offer?

THE DUTCHMAN

The price? Why even now I named the
price:
These are for shelter for a single
night!
Yet what you see is but the smallest
part
Of that which lies within my vessel's
hold.
What good's all this? I've never had a
wife
Or child, and I shall never find my
home!
All these my riches shall be yours if
you
Will let me have a home with you and
yours.

DALAND

What am I hearing?

THE DUTCHMAN

Do you have a daughter?

DALAND

Indeed, a loving child.

THE DUTCHMAN

Let her be mine!

DALAND

What? Is it true? He would have her
for wife?
He speaks his mind to me plainly!
I fear though, if I don't make up my
mind,
That he will withdraw his offer.
Well now, am I waking or sleeping?
Where's a son-in-law more to my mind?
A fool, if I forego such fortune.
I accept his offer with joy!

THE DUTCHMAN

Ah! Neither wife nor child have I,
Ties of this earth no more can bind me.

Rastlos verfolgt das Schicksal mich,
die Qual nur war mir Gefährte.
Nie werd' ich die Heimat erreichen:
was frommt mir der Güter Gewinn?
Lässt du zu dem Bund dich erweichen,
O! so nimm meine Schätze dahin!

DALAND

Wohl, Fremdling, hab' ich eine schöne
    Tochter,
mit treuer Kindeslieb' ergeben mir;
sie ist mein Stolz, das höchste meiner
    Güter,
mein Trost im Unglück, meine Freud'
    im Glück.

HOLLÄNDER

Dem Vater stets bewahr' sie ihre Liebe,
ihm treu, wird sie auch treu dem Gatten sein.

DALAND

Du gibst Juwelen, unschätzbare Perlen,
das höchste Kleinod doch, ein treues
Weib—

HOLLÄNDER

Du gibst es mir?

DALAND

Ich gebe dir mein Wort.
Mich rührt dein Los; freigebig, wie du
    bist,
zeigst Edelmut und hohen Sinn du mir:
Den Eidam wünscht' ich so; und wär'
    dein Gut
auch nicht so reich, wählt' ich doch
    keinen andren.

HOLLÄNDER

Hab' Dank! Werd' ich die Tochter
heut' noch seh'n?

DALAND

Der nächste günst'ge Wind bringt uns
    nach Haus;
du sollst sie sehn, und wenn sie dir ge-
fällt—

HOLLÄNDER

So ist sie mein . . .
Wird sie mein Engel sein?
Wenn aus der Qualen Schreckgewalten
die Sehnsucht nach dem Heil mich
    treibt,

ist mir's erlaubt, mich festzuhalten
an *einer* Hoffnung, die mir bleibt?
Darf ich in jenem Wahn noch schmach-
ten,
dass sich ein Engel mir erweicht?
Der Qualen, die mein Haupt umnach-
ten,
ersehntes Ziel hätt' ich erreicht?
Ach, ohne Hoffnung, wie ich bin,
geb' ich der Hoffnung doch mich hin!

DALAND

Gepriesen seid, des Sturm's Gewalten,
die ihr an diesen Strand mich triebt!
Fürwahr, bloss brauch' ich festzuhalten,
was sich so schön von selbst mir gibt.
Die ihn an diese Küste brachten,
ihr Winde, sollt gesegnet sein!
Ja, wonach alle Väter trachten,
ein reicher Eidam, er ist mein.
Ja, dem Mann mit Gut und hohem Sinn
geb' froh ich Haus und Tochter hin!

(*Der Sturm hat sich gänzlich gelegt;
der Wind ist umgeschlagen.*)

STEUERMANN

Südwind! Südwind!
Ach, lieber Südwind, blas noch mehr!

MATROSEN

Halloho! Hohohe! Hallojo!

DALAND

Du siehst, das Glück ist günstig dir:
der Wind ist gut, die See in Ruh'.
Sogleich die Anker lichten wir
und segeln schnell der Heimat zu.

STEUERMANN UND MATROSEN
(*die Anker lichtend und die
Segel aufspannend*)

Hoho! Hallojo!

HOLLÄNDER

Darf ich bitten, so segelst du voran;
der Wind ist frisch, doch meine Mannschaft müd.
Ich gönn' ihr kurze Ruh' und folge
dann.

DALAND

Doch, unser Wind?

HOLLÄNDER

Er bläst noch lang' aus Süd!
Mein Schiff ist schnell, es holt dich
sicher ein.

Fate has relentlessly followed me.
My one companion was torment.
I never shall get to my homeland,
So what's the good of wealth I have won?
But if this agreement finds favor,
Oh, then take all my treasure away!

DALAND

Well, stranger, yes, I have a lovely daughter,
Who gives her father faithful, filial love.
She is my pride, the best of my possessions,
In woe my comfort, and in weal my joy.

THE DUTCHMAN

And ever may her love rejoice her father!
Love shown to him means love to husband too.

DALAND

You offer jewels, pearls beyond all value,
But greater treasure yet is wife that's true . . .

THE DUTCHMAN

And she is mine?

DALAND

I give to you my word.
I grieve your fate. Free-handed as you are
You show to me your high and noble mind.
I'd want a son like you, and were your wealth
Not near so great, I still would choose no other.

THE DUTCHMAN

My thanks! And may I see the maid today?

DALAND

The next good wind will bring us to the house.
You'll see her there, and if she pleases you . . .

THE DUTCHMAN

Then she is mine . . . Is she my angel guide?
When from my torment's frightful power
The longing comes for cure and heal,
Still do I find one thing to cling to:

A sole, fond hope that yet remains.
Dare I indulge in folly's fancy,
That now an angel pities me?
And after all these crushing torments
Have I attained my longed-for goal?
Ah! Even though I have no hope,
I'll give myself to hope of hope!

DALAND

All praise to you, O storm, with your power,
For driving me upon this shore.
Indeed, I hardly need to grasp at
What fairly falls into my hand.
You winds that brought him to this seacoast,
Your happy deed be ever blest!
For such a son-in-law as every father
Seeks for, he is mine!
Yes, the man with wealth and noble mind
Shall take my house and daughter too!

(*The storm is over and the wind has changed.*)

STEERSMAN

Southwind! Southwind!
Ah, trusty southwind, blow some more.

SAILORS

Halloho! Hohohey!

DALAND

You see how fortune favors you:
The wind is fair, the sea is calm.
The anchor must be weighed straightway,
We swiftly sail for home today.

SAILORS

(*weighing anchor and setting sail*)
Hohohoho! Hallohe!

THE DUTCHMAN

If I dare ask you, sail on ahead of me;
The wind is fair, yet all my men are spent.
I'll let them rest a while and follow then.

DALAND

Yes, but our wind?

THE DUTCHMAN

It still comes from the south.
My ship is swift and soon will be ahead.

DALAND

Du glaubst? Wohlan, es möge denn so
sein!
Leb' wohl, mögst heute du mein Kind
noch sehn!

HOLLÄNDER

Gewiss!

DALAND

(an Bord seines Schiffes gehend)
Hei! Wie die Segel schon sich blähn!
Hallo! Hallo!
Frisch, Jungen, greifet an!

MATROSEN

Mit Gewitter und Sturm aus fernem
Meer—
mein Mädel bin dir nah! Hurra!
Über turmhohe Fluten vom Süden
her —
mein Mädel, ich bin da! Hurra!
Mein Mädel, wenn nicht Südwind wär',
ich nimmer wohl käm' zu dir:
Ach, lieber Südwind, blas noch mehr!
Mein Mädel verlangt nach mir.
Hohoho! Joloho!

(Der Holländer besteigt sein Schiff.)

ZWEITER AUFZUG

Ein geräumiges Zimmer im Hause Dalands.

*An den Seitenwänden Abbildungen von
Seegegenständen, Karten usw. An
der Wand im Hintergrunde das Bild
eines bleichen Mannes mit dunklem
Barte und in schwarzer Kleidung.—
Mary und die Mädchen sitzen um
den Kamin herum und spinnen;
Senta, in einem Grossvaterstuhl zu-
rückgelehnt und mit untergeschla-
genen Armen, ist im träumerischen
Anschauen des Bildes im Hintergrunde versunken.*

MÄDCHEN

Summ und brumm, du gutes Rädchen,
munter, munter, dreh' dich um!
Spinne, spinne tausend Fädchen,
gutes Rädchen, summ und brumm!
Mein Schatz ist auf dem Meere draus,
er denkt nach Haus
ans fromme Kind;
mein gutes Rädchen, braus und saus!
Ach! gäbst du Wind,
Er käm' geschwind.
Spinnt! Spinnt!
Fleissig, Mädchen!
Brumm! Summ!
Gutes Rädchen!

MARY

Ei! Fleissig, fleissig! Wie sie spinnen!
Will jede sich den Schatz gewinnen.

MÄDCHEN

Frau Mary, still! Denn wohl Ihr wisst,
das Lied noch nicht zu Ende ist.

MARY

So singt! Dem Rädchen lässt's nicht
Ruh'.
Du aber, Senta, schweigst dazu?

MÄDCHEN

Summ und brumm, du gutes Rädchen,
munter, munter, dreh' dich um!
Spinne, spinne tausend Fädchen,
gutes Rädchen, summ und brumm!
Mein Schatz, da draussen auf dem
Meer,
im Süden er
viel Gold gewinnt:
Ach, gutes Rädchen, saus noch mehr!
Er gibt's dem Kind,
wenn's fleissig spinnt.
Spinnt, spinnt!
Fleissig, Mädchen!
Brumm! Summ!
Gutes Rädchen!

MARY

(zu Senta)
Du böses Kind, wenn du nicht spinnst,
vom Schatz kein Geschenk gewinnst.

MÄDCHEN

Sie hat's nicht not, dass sie sich eilt;
ihr Schatz nicht auf dem Meere weilt.
Bringt er nicht Gold, bringt er doch
Wild —
man weiss ja, was ein Jäger gilt!
(Sie lachen.)
(Senta singt leise vor sich hin.)

MARY

Da seht ihr's! Immer vor dem Bild!
Willst du dein ganzes junges Leben
verträumen vor dem Konterfei?

SENTA

Was hast du Kunde mir gegeben,
was mir erzählet, wer er sei?
Der arme Mann!

MARY

Gott sei mit dir!

MÄDCHEN

Ei, ei! Ei, ei! Was hören wir!
Sie seufzet um den bleichen Mann!

DALAND

You say? All right, then let it be that way!
Farewell! I hope you see my child today.

THE DUTCHMAN

Indeed!

DALAND

(going on board his ship)

Hey! Even now the sails are swoll'n!
Hallo! Hallo! Up, laddies, to your work!

SAILORS

Through the lightning and storm from seas afar,
My sweetheart, I am near!
Over towering waves by southwind urged,
My sweetheart, I am here!
My sweetheart, if no southwind blew,
I'd never have come to you.
Ah, good man southwind, blow some more!
My sweetheart, she loves me true!
Hohoyo, hallohoho, yolloho, ho, ho!

(The Dutchman goes on)
board his ship.)

ACT TWO

A large room in Daland's house. On the walls, pictures of sea subjects, charts, etc. On the further wall the portrait of a pale man, with dark beard, in black Spanish garb.

(Mary and the maidens are sitting about the fireplace, spinning. Senta, leaning back in an armchair, is absorbed in dreamy contemplation of the portrait.)

MAIDENS

Hum and whir, good wheel, while twirling,
Cheerly, cheerly, turn around!
Spin a thousand threads while whirling,
Let the merry sounds abound!
My love is sailing far-off seas,
He thinks of home and offspring dear;
My trusty spinner, blow a breeze!
Ah! if you blew, he'd soon be here!
Spin, spin, be a winner!
Whirl, twirl, trusty spinner!

MARY

Ah! Swiftly, swiftly, how they're spinning!
Each girl a boy-friend would be winning!

MAIDENS

Dame Mary, hush! For well you know
The song we sing is not yet through!

MARY

Then sing! The spinning wheel won't rest.
You fancy, Senta, silence best?

MAIDENS

Hum and whir, good wheel, while twirling,
Cheerly, cheerly turn around!
Spin a thousand threads while whirling,
Let the merry sounds abound!
He sails afar whom I adore,
In southern climes much gold he wins;
Ah, trusty spinner, blow still more!
The prize is hers who swiftly spins!
Spin, spin, be a winner!
Whirl, twirl, trusty spinner!

MARY

(to Senta)

You naughty child, if you won't spin,
No lover's present will you win.

MAIDENS

She has no need to haste as we;
Her lover spends no time at sea.
He brings no gold, he brings her game;
He has no more than hunter's fame!
Ha ha ha ha ha ha ha!

(Senta sings softly to herself.)

MARY

You see her! Always staring there!
Why must you spend your whole life dreaming
Before that picture on the wall?

SENTA

Why have you told me of his sorrows?
Why have you told me who he is?
The hapless man!

MARY

God be with you!

MAIDENS

Ei, ei! Ei, ei! What's that we hear!
She's sighing for the spectre man!

MARY
Den Kopf verliert sie noch darum.

MÄDCHEN
Da sieht man, was ein Bild doch kann!

MARY
Nichts hilft es, wenn ich täglich
  brumm'!
Komm', Senta! Wend' dich doch herum!

MÄDCHEN
Sie hört Euch nicht—sie ist verliebt.
Ei, ei! Wenn's nur nicht Händel gibt.
Denn Erik hat gar heisses Blut—
dass er nur keinen Schaden tut!
Sagt nichts—er schiesst sonst, wutent-
  brannt,
den Nebenbuhler von der Wand.
  (*Sie lachen.*)

SENTA
(*heftig auffahrend*)
O schweigt! Mit eurem tollen Lachen
wollt ihr mich ernstlich böse machen?

MÄDCHEN
(*fallen sehr stark ein, indem sie die
Spinnräder heftig drehen, gleichsam,
um Senta nicht Zeit zum Schmälen
zu lassen*)
Summ und brumm! Du gutes Rädchen,
munter, munter dreh' dich um!
Spinne, spinne tausend Fädchen,
gutes Rädchen, summ und brumm!

SENTA
(*ärgerlich unterbrechend*)
O, macht dem dummen Lied ein Ende,
es brummt und summt mir vor dem
  Ohr!
Wollt ihr, dass ich mich zu euch wende,
so sucht' was Besseres hervor!

MÄDCHEN
Gut, singe du!

SENTA
Hört, was ich rate:
Frau Mary singt uns die Ballade.

MARY
Bewahre Gott! Das fehlte mir!
Den fliegenden Holländer lasst in Ruh'!

SENTA
Wie oft doch hört' ich sie von dir!
Ich sing' sie selbst! Hört, Mädchen, zu!
Lasst mich's euch recht zum Herzen
  führen:
Des Ärmsten Los, es muss euch rühren!

MÄDCHEN
Uns ist es recht.

SENTA
Merkt auf die Wort'!

MÄDCHEN
Dem Spinnrad Ruh'!

MARY
Ich spinne fort!

(*Mädchen rücken, nachdem sie ihre
Spinnräder beiseitegesetzt haben, die
Sitze dem Grossvaterstuhl näher und
gruppieren sich um Senta. Mary
spinnt fort.*)

SENTA
Johohoe! Johohohoe! Johoe!
Traft ihr das Schiff im Meere an,
blutrot die Segel, schwarz der Mast?
Auf hohem Bord der bleiche Mann,
des Schiffes Herr, wacht ohne Rast.
Hui! Wie saust der Wind! Johohe!
Hui! Wie pfeift's im Tau! Johohe!
Hui! Wie ein Pfeil fliegt er hin,
ohne Ziel, ohne Rast, ohne Ruh'!
Doch kann dem bleichen Manne Erlös-
  ung einstens noch werden,
fänd' er ein Weib, das bis in den Tod
  getreu ihm auf Erden!
Ach! Wann wirst du, bleicher See-
  mann, sie finden?
Betet zum Himmel, dass bald
ein Weib Treue ihm halt'!
Bei bösem Wind und Sturmes Wut
umsegeln wollt' er einst ein Kap;
er schwur und flucht' mit tollem Mut:
"In Ewigkeit lass' ich nicht ab!"
Hui! Und Satan hört's Johohe!
Hui! und nahm ihn beim Wort!
  Johohe!
Hui! Und verdammt zieht er nun
durch das Meer ohne Rast, ohne Ruh'!
Doch, dass der arme Mann noch Erlö-
  sung fände auf Erden,
zeigt Gottes Engel an, wie sein Heil ihm
  einst könne werden!
Ach! könntest du, bleicher Seemann, es
  finden!
Betet zum Himmel, dass bald
ein Weib Treue ihm halt'!
Vor Anker alle sieben Jahr',
ein Weib zu frein, geht er ans Land:
Er freite alle sieben Jahr',
noch nie ein treues Weib er fand.
Hui! "Die Segel auf!" Johohe!
Hui! "Den Anker los!" Johohe!
Hui! Falsche Lieb', falsche Treu'!
Auf in See, ohne Rast, ohne Ruh'!"

MARY

I think that she will lose her head!

MAIDENS

Just see now what a picture does!

MARY

I daily scold, but it's no use.
Come, Senta! Will you turn around?

MAIDENS

She hears you not! She is in love!
Ei, ei! I hope we have no scrape!
For Eric is of blood so hot,
I only hope he'll do no harm!
Don't talk! For if one stirs his gall
He'll shoot his rival from the wall!
Ha ha ha ha ha ha ha!

SENTA

(starting up angrily)

Be still! With all your silly laughing
D'you want to make me really angry?

MAIDENS

(sing and spin loudly to drown out
Senta's chiding)

Hum and whir, good wheel, while
   twirling,
Cheerly, cheerly turn around!
Spin a thousand threads while whirling,
Let the merry sounds abound!

SENTA

Oh, let this foolish song be ended,
Your whir and hum has numbed my
   ear.
If I'm to give you my attention,
Then find a better thing to hear!

MAIDENS

Good! Sing yourself!

SENTA

Hear my suggestion:
We'll let Dame Mary sing this ballad.

MARY

The Lord forbid! I really can't!
The Flying Dutchman leave in peace!

SENTA

I've often heard you sing the song!
I'll sing myself! So, maidens, hear!
Just let me touch your heart-strings
   truly:
His wretched lot will surely move you!

MAIDENS

All right with us!

SENTA

Mark well the words!

MAIDENS

We'll stop the wheels!

MARY

I'll spin away!
(The maidens move their seats nearer
   to the armchair, after they have put
   aside their spinning wheels, and
   group themselves round Senta. Mary
   goes on spinning.)

SENTA

Johohoe! Johohohoe! Hohohoe!
The ship is sailing ever on,
Blood red of sail and black of mast!
And on her deck the spectral man,
The vessel's lord, who never rests!
Hui! How howls the wind! Yohohey!
Hui! How creak the stays! Yohohey!
Hui! Like an arrow he flies,
Without aim, without stop, without
   rest!
Yet can the pallid man be redeemed
   and free from damnation
If he but find a woman who's true
   to bring him salvation!
Ah! When will you, pallid seaman,
   obtain her?
Pray then to heaven that soon a wife
   furnish this boon!
Through angry wind and tempest's
   roar
Around a cape he once would sail;
In foolish pride he cursed and swore:
" 'Spite God or devil I'll not fail!"
Hui! And Satan heard! Yohohey!
Hui! Took him at word! Yohohey!
Hui! And condemned, he must sail
   through the sea, without stop,
   without rest!
Yet, that the wretched man might
   achieve on earth his redemption,
God's angel showed him how from his
   woe to win his exemption!
Ah! That you might, pallid seaman,
   but find it!
Pray then to heaven that soon a
   wife furnish this boon!
He goes ashore each seven years,
In hope thereby to find a wife;
He woos one every seven years,
But finds none true in all his life.
Hui! Unfurl the sails! Yohohey!
Hui! And anchor up! Yohohey!
Hui! Faithless love! Faithless troth!
Back to sea, without stop, without rest!

MÄDCHEN

Ach! Wo weilt sie, die dir Gottes Engel
einst könnte zeigen?
Wo triffst du sie, die bis in den Tod
dein bliebe treueigen?

SENTA
(*springt vom Stuhle auf*)
Ich sei's, die dich durch ihre Treu'
erlöse!
Mög' Gottes Engel mich dir zeigen!
Durch mich sollst du das Heil erreichen!

MARY UND MÄDCHEN
Hilf, Himmel! Senta! Senta!

ERIK
(*ist zur Tür hereingetreten*)
Senta! Senta! Willst du mich verderben?

MÄDCHEN
Helft, Erik, uns! Sie ist von Sinnen!

MARY
Ich fühl' in mir das Blut gerinnen!
Abscheulich Bild, du sollst hinaus,
kommt nur der Vater erst nach Haus!

ERIK
Der Vater kommt!

SENTA
Der Vater kommt?

ERIK
Vom Felsen sah sein Schiff ich nah'n.

MARY
(*ausser sich, in grosser Geschäftigkeit*)
Nun seht, zu was eu'r Treiben frommt!
Im Hause ist noch nichts getan.

MÄDCHEN
Sie sind daheim! Auf, eilt hinaus!

MARY
Halt, halt! Ihr bleibet fein im Haus!
Das Schiffsvolk kommt mit leerem
Magen.
In Küch' und Keller! Säumet nicht!
Lasst euch nur von der Neugier
plagen—
vor allem geht an eure Pflicht!

MÄDCHEN (*für sich*)
Ach! Wie viel hab' ich ihn zu fragen!
Ich halte mich vor Neugier nicht.
Schon gut! Sobald nur aufgetragen,
hält hier uns länger keine Pflicht.
(*Mary treibt die Mädchen hinaus und
folgt ihnen.*)

ERIK
(*hält Senta zurück*)
Bleib', Senta! Bleib' nur einen Augenblick!
Aus meinen Qualen reisse mich! Doch
willst du,
Ach, so verdirb mich ganz!

SENTA
Was ist . . . ? Was soll?

ERIK
O Senta, sprich, was aus mir werden
soll?
Dein Vater kommt: eh' wieder er
verreist,
wird er vollbringen, was schon oft er
wollte . . .

SENTA
Und was meinst du?

ERIK
Dir einen Gatten geben.
Mein Herz, voll Treue bis zum Sterben,
mein dürftig Gut, mein Jägerglück:
Darf so um deine Hand ich werben?
Stösst mich dein Vater nicht zurück?
Wenn dann mein Herz im Jammer
bricht,
sag, Senta, wer dann für mich spricht?

SENTA
Ach, schweige, Erik, jetzt! Lass' mich
hinaus,
den Vater zu begrüssen!
Wenn nicht, wie sonst, an Bord die
Tochter kommt,
wird er nicht zürnen müssen?

ERIK
Du willst mich fliehn?

SENTA
Ich muss zum Port.

ERIK
Du weichst mir aus?

SENTA
Ach, lass mich fort!

ERIK
Fliehst du zurück vor dieser Wunde,
die du mir schlugst im Liebeswahn?
Ach, höre mich zu dieser Stunde,
hör' meine letzte Frage an;
Wenn dieses Herz im Jammer bricht,
wird's *Senta* sein, die für mich spricht?

MAIDENS

Ah, where is she, the one to whom
 heaven's angel might guide you?
Where may she dwell who's faithful to
 death, despite what betide you?

SENTA

(springing up from her chair)

Let me be she, who through her love
 will save you!
May heaven's angel guide you to me!
Through me at last you'll find
 salvation!

MARY AND MAIDENS

Heaven help us! Senta! Senta!

ERIC (entering)

Senta! Do you want to slay me?

MAIDENS

Help, Eric, help! She's lost her senses!

MARY

I feel the blood within course madly!
Abhorred picture, out you go,
Soon as her father comes back home!

ERIC

Her father comes!

SENTA

My father comes?

ERIC

From off the rock I saw his ship.

MARY

Now see what good your pother does!
There's nothing done yet in the house!

MAIDENS

They are at home! So hurry up!

MARY

Wait! Wait! You'd better stay right
 here!
The ship-folk come with empty stom-
 achs.
Fetch wine and victuals! Don't delay!
Restrain the urge to know that plagues
 you!
Before all else comes duty's task!

MAIDENS

Ah, how much do I have to ask him!
An urge within me wants to know.
Enough, as long as all is tidy,
We really have no further task.
 (Mary drives out the maidens
 and follows them.)

ERIC

(restraining Senta from leaving)

Wait, Senta! Wait for but a moment
 more!
And bring my torment to an end! Or
 will you,
Ah! thus destroy me quite!

SENTA

What's this? Just what?

ERIC

O Senta, speak, what will become of
 me?
Your father comes. Before he sails
 again
He will accomplish what he's long
 intended . . .

SENTA

And what is that?

ERIC

He seeks for you a husband!
My heart, so faithful, now and ever;
My straitened means, my hunter's
 lot,—
How dare I hope your hand will grace
 me?
Would not your father scorn the blot?
When then my heart in sorrow breaks,
Say, Senta, who then for me speaks?

SENTA

Ah! Silence, Eric, now! Let me go out:
I have to greet my father.
Unless I go on board, as other times,
I know he'll be quite angry.

ERIC

You run from me?

SENTA

Just to the port.

ERIC

You shrink from me?

SENTA

Oh, let me go!

ERIC

Why do you flee the wound you give
 me,
After it pains my loving heart?
Ah! Hear my fond, final pleading
 question,
Hear what I ask, before we part!
When my poor heart in sorrow breaks,
Will you be she who for me speaks?

SENTA

Wie? Zweifelst du an meinem Herzen?
Du zweifelst, ob ich gut dir bin?
O, sag, was weckt dir solche Schmer-
zen?
Was trübt mit Argwohn deinen Sinn?

ERIK

Dein Vater, ach!—nach Schätzen
geizt er nur . . .
Und Senta, du? Wie dürft' auf dich
ich zählen?
Erfülltest du nur *eine* meiner Bitten?
Kränkst du mein Herz nicht jeden
Tag?

SENTA

Dein Herz?

ERIK

Was soll ich denken? Jenes Bild . . .

SENTA

Das Bild?

ERIK

Lasst du von deiner Schwärmerei wohl
ab?

SENTA

Kann meinem Blick Teilnahme ich
verwehren?

ERIK

Und die Ballade—heut noch sangst du
sie!

SENTA

Ich bin ein Kind und weiss nicht, was
ich singe . . .
O, sag', wie? Fürchtest du ein Lied,
ein Bild?

ERIK

Du bist so bleich . . . sag', sollte ich's
nicht fürchten?

SENTA

Soll mich des Ärmsten Schreckenslos
nicht rühren?

ERIK

Mein Leiden, Senta, rührt es dich nicht
mehr?

SENTA

O prahle nicht! Was kann *dein* Leiden
sein?
Kennst jenes Unglücksel'gen Schicksal
du?
Fühlst du den Schmerz, den tiefen
Gram,
mit dem herab er auf mich sieht?
Ach, was die Ruhe für ewig ihm nahm,
wie schneidend Weh durchs Herz mir
zieht!

ERIK

Weh mir! Es mahnt mich mein unsel'ger Traum!
Gott schütze dich! Satan hat dich um-
garnt!

SENTA

Was schreckt dich so?

ERIK

Senta! Lass dir vertraun:
ein Traum ist's! Hör ihn zu Warnung
an!
Auf hohem Felsen lag ich träumend,
sah unter mir des Meeres Flut;
die Brandung hört' ich, wie sie schäu-
mend
am Ufer brach der Wogen Wut.
Ein fremdes Schiff am nahen Strande
erblickt' ich seltsam, wunderbar;
zwei Männer nahten sich dem Lande,
der ein', ich sah's, dein Vater war.

SENTA

Der andre?

ERIK

Wohl erkannt' ich ihn;
mit schwarzem Wams, die bleiche
Mien' . . .

SENTA

Der düstre Blick . . .

ERIK

(auf das Bild deutend)

Der Seemann, er.

SENTA

Und ich?

ERIK

Du kamst vom Hause her,
du flogst, den Vater zu begrüssen,
doch kaum noch sah ich an dich langen,
du stürztest zu des Fremden Füssen —
ich sah dich seine Knie umfangen . . .

SENTA

Er hub mich auf . . .

ERIK

An seine Brust;
voll Inbrunst hingst du dich an ihn—
du küsstest ihn mit heisser Lust—

SENTA

Und dann?

ERIK

Sah ich aufs Meer euch fliehn.

SENTA

Er sucht mich auf! Ich muss ihn sehn!
Mit ihm muss ich zugrunde gehn!

SENTA

What? Do you doubt my heart's devo-
tion,
Or doubt my thought to you is kind?
Oh, tell what wakes this pained emo-
tion,
What vain suspicion clouds your mind?

ERIC

Your father, ah! He's greedy but for
gold!
And Senta, you, are you the one to
count on?
When have you ever granted what I
asked for?
Do you not wound my heart each day?

SENTA

Your heart?

ERIC

Must I not wonder? Yonder face . . .

SENTA

That face?

ERIC

Why not give up your wild and foolish
dreams?

SENTA

How can my face not show my heart's
compassion?

ERIC

And then, the ballad, sung by you
today!

SENTA

I am a child, and know not what I'm
singing!
Oh say, come? Do you fear a song, a
face?

ERIC

You are so pale, say, should I not be
fearful?

SENTA

Should not that poor man's fearful
fate affect me?

ERIC

My sorrow, Senta, does it move you
less?

SENTA

Oh, do not brag! What can your sor-
row be?
What can you know of that poor
wretch's fate?
Do you feel the pain, the deep distress
Within the look he turns on me?
Ah! how the doom that demolished his
rest
Has sharply pierced my inmost heart!

ERIC

Woe's me! I think on my unhappy
dream!
God guard you well! You are in Satan's
toils!

SENTA

What affrights you so?

ERIC

Senta, I had a dream.
I'll tell it! Pay heed and let it warn!
On rocky height I lay a-dreaming;
Below I saw the swelling sea.
I heard the breakers, as in anger
They dashed in foam against the shore.
I saw a foreign ship approaching
The mainland, awesome, wonderful!
Two seamen stood within the vessel.
And then I saw your father's face.

SENTA

The other?

ERIC

Well I knew the man:
With doublet black, and pallid face . . .

SENTA

The mournful look . . .

ERIC (*pointing*)

The seaman, he.

SENTA

And I?

ERIC

I saw you leave the house,
You went in haste to greet your father.
I saw when you had barely reached
them
You cast yourself before the stranger.
Around his knees I saw you clasp
him . . .

SENTA

He raised me up . . .

ERIC

Yes, to his breast.
You hung on him most fervently.
You kissed him too with hot desire.

SENTA

And then?

ERIC

You both fled out to sea.

SENTA

He seeks me out! For him I look!
With him, surely, I'll share his doom!

ERIK

Entsetzlich! Ha, mir wird es klar!
Sie ist dahin! Mein Traum sprach
wahr!

(*Er stürzt voll Entsetzen ab.*)

SENTA

Ach, möchtest du, bleicher Seemann,
sie finden!
Betet zum Himmel, dass bald
ein Weib Treue ihm . . . Ha!

(*Die Tür geht auf. Daland und der
Holländer treten ein. Sentas Blick
streift vom Bilde auf den Holländer,
sie stösst einen Schrei der Überrasch-
ung aus und bleibt wie festgebannt
stehen, ohne ihr Auge vom Holländer
abzuwenden. Der Holländer geht
langsam in den Vordergrund.*)

DALAND

(*nachdem er an der Schwelle stehen-
geblieben, näher tretend*)

Mein Kind, du siehst mich auf der
Schwelle . . .
Wie? Kein Umarmen? Keinen Kuss?
Du bleibst gebannt an deiner Stelle—
verdien' ich, Senta, solchen Gruss?

SENTA

(*Als Daland bei ihr anlangt, ergreift sie
seine Hand, ihn näher an sich
ziehend.*)

Gott dir zum Gruss!
Mein Vater, sprich!
Wer ist der Fremde?

DALAND

Drängst du mich?
Mögst du, mein Kind, den fremden
Mann willkommen heissen;
Seemann ist er gleich mir, das Gast-
recht spricht er an.
Lang' ohne Heimat, stets auf fernen,
weiten Reisen,
in fremden Landen er der Schätze viel
gewann.
Aus seinem Vaterland verwiesen,
für einen Herd er reichlich lohnt:
Sprich, Senta, würd' es dich verdriessen,
wenn dieser Fremde bei uns wohnt?

(*Daland wendet sich zum Holländer.*)

Sagt, hab' ich sie zuviel gepriesen?
Ihr seht sie selbst—ist sie Euch recht?
Soll ich von Lob noch überfliessen?
Gesteht, sie zieret ihr Geschlecht!

(*Der Holländer macht eine
Bewegung des Beifalls.*)

Mögst du, mein Kind, dem Manne
freundlich dich erweisen!
Von deinem Herzen auch spricht holde
Gab' er an;
reich ihm die Hand, denn Bräutigam
sollst du ihn heissen:
stimmst du dem Vater bei, ist morgen
er dein Mann.

(*Daland zieht einen Schmuck hervor
und zeigt ihn seiner Tochter.*)

Sieh dieses Band, sieh diese Spangen!
Was er besitzt, macht dies gering.
Muss, teures Kind, dich's nicht verlan-
gen?
Dein ist es, wechselst du den Ring.

(*Senta, ohne ihn zu beachten, wendet
ihren Blick nicht vom Holländer ab,
sowie auch dieser, nur in den Anblick
des Mädchens versunken ist.*)

Doch keines spricht . . . Sollt' ich hier
lästig sein?
So ist's! Am besten lass' ich sie allein.

(*zu Senta*)

Mögst du den edlen Mann gewinnen!
Glaub mir, solch Glück wird nimmer
neu.

(*zum Holländer*)

Bleibt hier allein! Ich geh' von hinnen:
Glaubt mir, wie schön, so ist sie treu!

(*Er geht langsam ab, indem er die
beiden verwundert betrachtet.*)

HOLLÄNDER

Wie aus der Ferne längst vergangner
Zeiten
spricht dieses Mädchens Bild zu mir:
Wie ich's geträumt seit bangen Ewig-
keiten,
vor meinen Augen seh' ich's hier—
Wohl hub auch ich voll Sehnsucht
mein Blicke
aus tiefer Nacht empor zu einem Weib:
Ein schlagend Herz liess, ach! mir Satans Tücke,
dass eingedenk ich meiner Qualen
bleib'.
Die düstre Glut, die hier ich fühle brennen,
sollt' ich Unseliger sie Liebe nennen?
Ach nein! Die Sehnsucht ist es nach
dem Heil:
Würd' es durch solchen Engel mir
zuteil!

SENTA

Versank ich *jetzt* in wunderbares Träu-
men,

ERIC

How frightful! Now all is clear!
I know she's lost! My dream was true!

(*He rushes away in horror
and despair.*)

SENTA

Ah! When will you, pallid seaman,
obtain her?
Pray then to heaven that soon a wife
furnish this . . .

(*The door opens. The Dutchman and
Daland appear. Senta's gaze turns
from the picture to him. She utters
a cry and remains standing spell-
bound, without removing her eyes
from the Dutchman, who walks to-
wards Senta, his eyes fixed on her.*)

DALAND

(*remains standing at the door, but
when Senta fails to approach him he
approaches her*)

My child, you see me on the threshold.
Well? No embraces? Nor a kiss?
You stand as though you were a
statue.
Is this my greeting when I come?

SENTA

(*seizing his hand and drawing*)
him nearer)

God greet you here! My father, speak!
Who is the stranger?

DALAND

Would you know?
Can you, my child, give kindly wel-
come to this stranger?
Seaman is he, like me, and asks to be
our guest.
Long without homeland, always roam-
ing distant waters,
From far-off climes he's won much
treasure for his chest.
He lives in exile from his country,
And for a hearth will richly pay.
Well, Senta, would it much disturb you
Should such a stranger with us stay?

(*to the Dutchman*)

Say, have I praised her over-highly?
You see her now, is she not fair?
Shall I continue pouring praises?
Confess, is she not past compare?

(*The Dutchman nods. Daland
turns again to Senta.*)

Will you, my child, show friendly favor
to the stranger?
He asks a gracious gift, a heart that's
kindly bred.
Give him your hand, it is yours to call
him bridegroom.
If of your father's mind, tomorrow you
will wed.

(*He shows Senta some jewelry.*)

Look on this band, look on these
bracelets!
To what he owns these are but toys.
Dear child, you surely must desire
them.
Exchange your ring and these are
yours!

(*Senta pays no attention. She and the
Dutchman are staring at each other.*)

Yet neither speaks. Why should I
weary them?
I know. It's best I leave them both
alone.

(*to Senta*)

May you obtain this noble husband!
Luck such as this will not come twice!

(*to the Dutchman*)

Stay here alone! I'm going to leave you.
Know it: she's true as she is fair.

(*He slowly departs, watching the two
the while.*)

THE DUTCHMAN

As if from out a dim and distant past
This fair maiden's picture speaks to me.
Just as I dreamed through long and
fearful ages,
Such is she now before my eyes.
Yes, I have dared to raise a look of
longing
Through depths of night and up unto a
maid.
My beating heart remained, through
Satan's malice,
That I might hold remembrance of my
pain!
O wretched man, is love the name that
I should give
To the sullen glow that burns within
me?
Ah no! My longing is for healing balm.
Would this might come through angel
such as she!

SENTA

And am I lost in depths of wondrous
dreaming?

was ich *erblicke,* ist es Wahn?
Weilt' ich *bisher* in trügerischen Räumen,
brach des *Erwachens* Tag heut an?
Er steht vor mir mit leidenvollen Zügen,
es spricht sein unerhörter Gram zu mir:
Kann tiefen Mitleids Stimme mich belügen?
Wie ich ihn oft gesehn, so steht er hier.
Die Schmerzen, die in meinem Busen brennen,
Ach! dies Verlangen, wie soll ich es nennen?
Wonach mit Sehnsucht es dich treibt—das Heil,
würd' es, du Ärmster, dir durch mich zuteil!

HOLLÄNDER

Wirst du des Vaters Wahl nicht schelten?
Was er versprach, wie?—dürft' es gelten?
Du könntest dich für ewig mir ergeben
und deine Hand dem Fremdling reichtest du?
Soll finden ich nach qualenvollem Leben
in deiner Treu' die langersehnte Ruh'?

SENTA

Wer du auch seist und welches das Verderben,
dem grausam dich dein Schicksal konnte weihn—
was auch das Los, das ich mir sollt' erwerben:
Gehorsam stets werd' ich dem Vater sein!

HOLLÄNDER

So unbedingt, wie? könnte dich durchdringen
für meine Leiden tiefstes Mitgefühl?

SENTA

(halb für sich)

O, welche Leiden! Könnt' ich Trost dir bringen!

HOLLÄNDER

Welch holder Klang im nächtlichen Gewühl!
Du bist ein Engel! Eines Engels Liebe
Verworfne selbst zu trösten weiss.
O, wenn Erlösung mir zu hoffen bliebe,
Allewiger, durch *diese* sei's!

SENTA

Ach, wenn Erlösung ihm zu hoffen bliebe,
Allewiger, durch *mich* nur sei's!

HOLLÄNDER

O, könntest das Geschick du ahnen,
dem dann mit mir du angehörst,
dich würd' es an das Opfer mahnen,
das du mir bringst, wenn Treu' du schwörst.
Es flöhe schaudernd deine Jugend
dem Lose, dem du sie willst weihn,
nennst du des Weibes schönste Tugend,
nennst ew'ge Treue du nicht dein!

SENTA

Wohl kenn' ich Weibes heil'ge Pflichten,
sei drum getrost, unsel'ger Mann!
Lass über *die* das Schicksal richten,
die seinem Spruche trotzen kann!
In meines Herzens höchster Reine
kenn' ich der Treue Hochgebot:
wem ich sie weih', schenk' ich die *eine,*
die Treue bis zum Tod!

HOLLÄNDER

Ein heil'ger Balsam meinen Wunden
dem Schwur, dem hohen Wort entfliesst.
Hört es, mein Heil hab' ich gefunden,
Mächte, die ihr zurück mich stiesst!
Du, Stern des Unheils, sollst erblassen,
Licht meiner Hoffnung, leuchte neu!
Ihr Engel, die mich einst verlassen,
stärkt jetzt dies Herz in seiner Treu'!

SENTA

Von mächt'gem Zauber überwunden,
reisst mich's zu seiner Rettung fort:
Hier habe Heimat er gefunden,
Hier ruh' sein Schiff in sichrem Port!
Was ist's, das mächtig in mir lebet?
Was schliesst berauscht mein Busen ein?
Allmächt'ger, was mich so hoch erhebet,
lass'es die Kraft der Treue sein.

DALAND

(wieder eintretend)

Verzeiht! Mein Volk hält draussen sich nicht mehr;

Do I imagine what I see?
Have I till now been dwelling in a
 dreamland?
Has day of wakening only dawned?
He stands right here, his features full
 of sorrow;
He tells a tale of unexampled woe.
Can deep-felt pity's voice so badly
 cheat me?
As I have seen him oft, so stands he
 here.
The sorrow which within my breast is
 burning
Ah! with its yearning, what am I to call
 it?
The goal that draws you on and on,
 that balm,
Poor man, I wish it might be found
 through me!

THE DUTCHMAN

Will you approve your father's
 judgment?
His promise made, well, is it valid?
Could you allot yourself to me
 forever
And reach your hand to stranger like
 myself?
Say, shall I find, with time of torment
 ended,
Within your love, my long-awaited
 rest?

SENTA

Whoso you be, no matter what
 destruction
A cruel fate may have in store for you,
No matter what the lot that I inherit,
I always shall obey my father's will.

THE DUTCHMAN

Without reserve! Well! Could it be, my
 sorrows
Have pierced your heart to deepest
 pity's pang?

SENTA (aside)

Oh, what affliction! Oh, if I could
 comfort!

THE DUTCHMAN

What grateful sound to end my night of
 woe!
You are an angel, and the love of
 angels
Can comfort even one who's lost!
Ah, if redemption may be mine to hope
 for,
Almighty, grant that she may save!

SENTA

Ah! If redemption may be his to hope
 for,
Almighty, grant that I may save!

THE DUTCHMAN

Ah, were you but to view the future
Which you would share with me, when
 mine,
You'd think about the step you're
 taking
In making such great sacrifice.
Your youth would, shuddering, flee that
 lot
Most untoward, which you soon would
 find,
Were not a woman's fairest virtues,
Truth, faith and honor, deep within!

SENTA

Well do I know those holy duties;
So be consoled, unhappy man!
Let fate on those expend its judgment
Who dare defy its stern decrees!
Within my heart's most holy chambers
Lies locked the sacred law of truth.
One has my oath. Here do I pledge
 him:
My honor until death!

THE DUTCHMAN

My wounds have found a holy balsam,
Her oath, outpoured in noble words!
Hear this, my cure at last is granted.
Hear me, you powers who once did
 drive me back!
You, star of evil, now are waning!
Bright hope of heaven, shine anew!
You angel, you who once forsook me,
Make strong this heart, and keep it
 firm.

SENTA

Some mighty magic has involved me,
Making me his deliverer.
Here may he find at last his homeland,
Here may his ship find quiet port!
What mighty power lives within me?
What heady feeling stirs my breast?
Almighty, Thou who raisest my spirit,
Grant me Thy strength, that I be true!

DALAND (reentering)

I say! My men will no longer wait
 outside;

nach jeder Rückkunft, wisset, gibt's ein Fest:
verschönern möcht' ich's, komme deshalb her,
ob mit Verlobung sich's vereinen lässt?
(*zum Holländer*)
Ich denk', Ihr habt nach Herzenswunsch gefreit?
Senta, mein Kind, sag', bist auch du bereit?

SENTA
Hier meine Hand! Und ohne Reu'
bis in den Tod gelob' ich Treu'!

HOLLÄNDER
Sie reicht die Hand! Gesprochen sei
Hohn, Hölle, dir durch ihre Treu'!

DALAND
Euch soll dies Bündnis nicht gereun!
Zum Fest! Heut soll sich alles freun!

(*Alle ab*)

DRITTER AUFZUG
Seebucht mit felsigem Gestade.
Das Haus Dalands zur Seite im Vordergrunde. Den Hintergrund nehmen die beiden Schiffe, das des Norwegers und das des Holländers, ein. Helle Nacht. Das norwegische Schiff ist erleuchtet; die Matrosen desselben sind auf dem Verdeck. Jubel und Freude. Die Haltung des holländischen Schiffes bietet einen unheimlichen Kontrast: eine unnatürliche Finsternis und Totenstille ist über dasselbe ausgebreitet.

MATROSEN DES NORWEGERS
Steuermann, lass die Wacht!
Steuermann, her zu uns!
Ho! He! Je! Ha!
Hisst die Segel auf! Anker fest!
Steuermann, her!
Fürchten weder Wind noch bösen Strand,
wollen heute 'mal recht lustig sein!
Jeder hat sein Mädel auf dem Land,
herrlichen Tabak und guten Branntewein.
Hussassahe!
Klipp' und Sturm draus—
Jollohohe!
Lachen wir aus!
Hussassahe!
Segel ein! Anker fest! Klipp' und Sturm lachen wir aus!
Steuermann, lass die Wacht!
Steuermann, her zu uns!
Ho! He! Je! Ha!

Steuermann, her! Trink mit uns!
(*Sie tanzen auf dem Verdeck. Die Mädchen kommen mit Körben voll Speisen und Getränken.*)

MÄDCHEN
Mein! Seht doch an! Sie tanzen gar!
Der Mädchen bedarf's da nicht fürwahr.
(*Sie gehen auf das holländische Schiff zu.*)

MATROSEN
He! Mädel! Halt! Wo geht ihr hin?

MÄDCHEN
Steht euch nach frischem Wein der Sinn?
Eu'r Nachbar dort soll auch was haben!
Ist Trank und Schmaus für euch allein?

STEUERMANN
Fürwahr! Tragt's hin den armen Knaben!
Vor Durst sie scheinen matt zu sein!

MATROSEN
Man hört sie nicht!

STEUERMANN
Ei, seht doch nur!
Kein Licht! Von der Mannschaft keine Spur!

MÄDCHEN
He! Seeleut'! He! Wollt Fackeln ihr?
Wo seid ihr doch? Man sieht nicht hier!

MATROSEN
Hahaha!
Weckt sie nicht auf! Sie schlafen noch.

MÄDCHEN
He! Seeleut'! He! Antwortet doch!
(*grosse Stille*)

STEUERMAN UND MATROSEN
Haha!
Wahrhaftig! Sie sind tot:
Sie haben Speis' und Trank nicht not!

MÄDCHEN
(*in das Schiff hineinrufend*)
Wie, Seeleute? Liegt ihr so faul schon im Nest?
Ist heute für euch denn nicht auch ein Fest?

MATROSEN
Sie liegen fest auf ihrem Platz,
wie Drachen hüten sie den Schatz.

MÄDCHEN
He, Seeleute! Wollt ihr nicht frischen Wein?

You know, we banquet after every
 trip.
I would enhance this, therefore I have
 come,
Wondering if you would join your
 feast to ours?

(*to the Dutchman*)

I think that you have wooed to heart's
 content?
Senta, my child, say, are you ready too?

SENTA

Here is my hand, without regret;
Here, until death, I plight my troth!

THE DUTCHMAN

She gives her hand! Defiance to you,
Powers of hell, through power of truth!

DALAND

You'll not regret your marriage vows!
The feast! All shall rejoice today.

ACT THREE

*A bay with rocky shore. Daland's house
in foreground. Two ships, Daland's
and the Dutchman's, in the back-
ground. The night is clear. The Norwegian ship is lighted up.*

(*The sailors are making merry on the
deck. But the Dutch ship is dark and
silent.*)

NORWEGIAN SAILORS

Steersman, leave the watch!
Steersman, come to us!
Ho, He, Hey, Ha!
Time to hoist the sails! Anchor fast!
Steersman, come!
Fearing neither storm nor rocky strand,
On this day let's have a jolly time!
Sailors have their sweeties on the land!
Good tobacco's free, and best of brandy-
 wine!
Hussassahey!
Reefs and storms, bah!
Hallohohey!
That's to laugh, ha!
Hussassahey!
Furl the sails! Anchor fast! Reefs and
 storms,
They're a laugh! Ha!
Steersman, come, drink with us!

(*They dance on the deck. The maidens
come out of the house, carrying
baskets with food and liquors.*)

MAIDENS

Hey, take a look! They dance, indeed!
Of girls, though, they seem to have no
 need!

(*They go toward the Dutch ship.*)

SAILORS

Hey! Sweethearts! Stop! Where do you
 go?

MAIDENS

Well, would you like some sparkling
 wine?
Your neighbors there must also crave
 some!
Are food and drink for you alone?

STEERSMAN

Of course, so let the poor lads have
 some!
They seem to be quite faint with thirst,
 quite faint!

SAILORS

There's not a sound!

STEERSMAN

Ei, see the place!
No light! Of the seamen not a trace!

MAIDENS

Hey, sailors! Hey, need lights in
 there?
Where are they then? It's dark in
 here!

SAILORS

Ha ha ha! Don't wake them up!
Asleep they loll!

MAIDENS

Hey! Sailors! Hey! Answer our call!

(*deep silence*)

STEERSMAN AND SAILORS

Haha! Most surely, they are dead.
They have no need of wine or bread.

MAIDENS

(*calling to the Dutch ship*)

Hey, sailors and sluggards, why so soon
 asleep?
Is this not a day that you too should
 keep?

SAILORS

They sleep most soundly in the hold,
Like dragons brooding over gold.

MAIDENS

Hey, sea laddies, won't you have
 sparkling wine?

Ihr müsset wahrlich doch durstig auch
sein!

MATROSEN

Sie trinken nicht, sie singen nicht;
in ihrem Schiffe brennt kein Licht.

MÄDCHEN

Sagt! Habt ihr denn nicht auch ein
Schätzchen am Land?
Wollt ihr nicht mit tanzen auf freund-
lichem Strand?

MATROSEN

Sie sind schon alt und bleich statt rot!
Und ihre Liebsten, die sind tot!

MÄDCHEN

He! Seeleut'! Seeleut'! Wacht doch
auf!
Wir bringen euch Speise und Trank zu
Hauf!

MATROSEN

He! Seeleut'! Seeleut'! Wacht doch
auf!

(langes Stillschweigen)

MÄDCHEN

Wahrhaftig, ja! Sie scheinen tot.
Sie haben Speis' und Trank nicht not.

MATROSEN

Vom fliegenden Holländer wisst ihr ja!
Sein Schiff, wie es leibt, wie es lebt, seht
ihr da!

MÄDCHEN

So weckt die Mannschaft ja nicht auf:
Gespenster sind's, wir schwören drauf!

MATROSEN

Wieviel hundert Jahre seid ihr zur See?
Euch tut ja der Sturm und die Klippe
nicht weh!

MÄDCHEN

Sie trinken nicht! Sie singen nicht!
In ihrem Schiffe brennt kein Licht.

MATROSEN

Habt ihr keine Brief', keine Aufträg'
für's Land?
Unsren Urgrossvätern wir bringen's zur
Hand!

MÄDCHEN

Sie sind schon alt und bleich statt rot!
Und ihre Liebsten, ach, sind tot!

MATROSEN

Hei, Seeleute! Spannt eure Segel doch
auf
und zeigt uns des fliegenden Holländers
Lauf!

MÄDCHEN

(sich mit ihren Körben furchtsam vom
holländischen Schiffe entfernend)
Sie hören nicht! Uns graust es hier!
Sie wollen nichts—was rufen wir?

MATROSEN

Ihr Mädel, lasst die Toten ruhn!
Lasst's uns Lebend'gen gütlich tun!

MÄDCHEN

(den Matrosen ihre Körbe über
Bord reichend)
So nehmt! Der Nachbar hat's ver-
schmäht.

STEUERMANN

Wie? Kommt ihr denn nicht selbst an
Bord?

MÄDCHEN

Ei, jetzt noch nicht! Es ist ja nicht spät!
Wir kommen bald! Jetzt trinkt nur fort,
und, wenn ihr wollt, so tanzt dazu,
nur gönnt dem müden Nachbar Ruh'.

MATROSEN (die Körbe leerend)

Juchhe! Juchhe! Da gibt's die Fülle!
Lieb' Nachbar, habe Dank!

STEUERMANN

Zum Rand sein Glas ein jeder fülle!
Lieb' Nachbar liefert uns den Trank.

MATROSEN

Hallohohoho!
Lieb' Nachbarn, habt ihr Stimm' und
Sprach',
so wachet auf und macht's uns nach!
Steuermann, lass die Wacht!
Steuermann, her zu uns!
Ho! He! Je! Ha!
Hisst die Segel auf! Anker fest!
Steuermann her!
Wachten manche Nacht bei Sturm und
Graus,
tranken oft des Meeres gesalznes Nass:
Heute wachen wir bei Saus und
Schmaus,
Besseres Getränk gibt Mädel uns vom
Fass.
Hussassahe!
Klipp' und Sturm draus'.
Jollohohe!

Surely for thirsty folk, wine would be
fine.

SAILORS

To drink or sing they have no might,
Within their ship there burns no light.

MAIDENS

Say, do you not have any girl-friends
on land?
Why do you not join us and dance on
the strand?

SAILORS

They all are old, and pale, not red;
As for their girl-friends, they are dead.

MAIDENS

Hey! Seafolk! Seafolk! Wake up there!
We bring you food and drink to spare!

SAILORS

They bring you food and drink to
spare!
(long silence)

MAIDENS

We think so, yes! Most dead, indeed!
Of food and drink they have no need.

SAILORS

The Flying Dutchman, you've heard
about;
You're seeing his ship large as life,
do not doubt.

MAIDENS

We must not try to wake the crew,
For they are spooks, we know it's
true!

SAILORS

You've been on the sea now for
hundreds of years.
Of dangerous storm and the rocks
you've no fears.

MAIDENS

To drink or sing they have no might,
Within their ship there burns no light.

SAILORS

Have you no commission or letter for
land
To be brought to our great-great-grand-
father's hand?

MAIDENS

They all are old, and pale, not red;
As for their girl-friends, they are dead.

SAILORS

Hey! Seapeople, spread out your sails
for your trip,
And show how your Flying Dutchman
can rip!

MAIDENS

*(retreating with alarm from the neigh-
borhood of the Dutch ship)*
They hear us not! We shake with fear!
They want us not! Why dally here?

SAILORS

You sweethearts, give the dead a rest!
Let us who live enjoy the best!

MAIDENS

(reaching baskets to sailors)
Take this! Your neighbor turned it
down!

STEERSMEN AND SAILORS

How? Why not come on board your-
selves?

MAIDENS

No, not right now, the night is quite
young.
We'll come back soon, now drink away,
And if you will, go dance with zest,
But grant your weary neighbors rest!

SAILORS

(opening and emptying baskets)
Hurrah! We sure have plenty!
Dear neighbors, take our thanks!

STEERSMAN

Let each man pour a brimming
bumper!
Good neighbors, let us down your
drink!

SAILORS

Halloho! Halloho! Ho, ho, ho!
Good neighbors, you can speak aloud,
So wake up now and join our crowd!
Steersman, leave the watch!
Steersman, here to us!
Ho, hey, yay, hah!
Hoist the sails right up! Anchor fast!
Steersman, here!
We have often watched through storms
that rage,
We have often drunk the briny spray;
This time though our watch wins nicer
wage,
Better is the drink our sweeties give
away!

*(Das Meer, das sonst überall ruhig
bleibt, hat sich im Umkreise des
holländischen Schiffes zu heben beg-
onnen; eine düstere, bläuliche Flam-
me lodert in diesem als Wachtfeuer
auf. Sturmwind erhebt sich in dessen
Tauen. Die Mannschaft, von der
man zuvor nichts sah, belebt sich.)*

MANNSCHAFT DES HOLLÄNDERS
Johohoe! Johohoe! Hoe! Hoe! Hoe!
Hui—ssa!
Nach dem Land treibt der Sturm
Hui—ssa!
Segel ein! Anker los!
In die Bucht laufet ein!
Schwarzer Hauptmann, geh ans Land,
sieben Jahre sind vorbei!
Frei' um blonden Mädchens Hand!
Blondes Mädchen, sei ihm treu!
Lustig heut, hui!
Bräutigam! Hui!
Sturmwind heult Brautmusik—Ozean
tanzt dazu!
Hui! Horch, er pfeift!
Kapitän, bist wieder da?
Hui! Segel auf!
Deine Braut, sag, wo sie blieb?
Hui! Auf, in See!
Kapitän! Kapitän! Hast kein Glück in
der Lieb'!
Hahaha!
Sause, Sturmwind, heute zu!
Unsren Segeln lässt du Ruh'!
Satan hat sie uns gefeit,
reissen nicht in Ewigkeit.
Hohoe! nicht in Ewigkeit!

*(Während des Gesanges der Holländer
wird ihr Schiff von den Wogen auf
und ab getragen; furchtbarer Sturmwind heult und pfeift durch die
Taue. Die Luft und das Meer bleiben,
ausser in der nächsten Umgebung
des holländischen Schiffes, ruhig
wie zuvor.)*

MATROSEN DES NORWEGERS
Welcher Sang? Ist es Spuk? Wie mich's
graut!
Stimmet an—unser Lied! Singet laut!
Steuermann, lass die Wacht!
Steuermann, her zu uns!
Ho! He! Je! Ha!

*(Das Tosen des Meeres, das Sausen,
Heulen und Pfeifen des unnatür-
lichen Sturmes sowie der immer
wilder werdende Gesang der Holländer bringt die Norweger zum
Schweigen. Sie schlagen das Kreuz
und verlassen das Verdeck; die Hol-*

*länder erheben ein gellendes Hohn-
gelächter. Sodann herrscht mit einem
Mal auf ihrem Schiffe wieder Totenstille; Luft und Meer werden ruhig,
wie zuvor. Senta kommt bewegten
Schrittes aus dem Hause; ihr folgt
Erik in höchster Aufregung.)*

ERIK
Was musst' ich hören, Gott, was musst'
ich sehen!
Ist's Täuschung, Wahrheit? Ist es Tat?

SENTA
*(sich mit peinlichem Gefühle
abwendend)*
O, frage nicht! Antwort darf ich nicht
geben.

ERIK
Gerechter Gott! Kein Zweifel! Es ist
wahr!
Welch unheilvolle Macht riss dich
dahin?
Welche Macht verführte dich so schnell,
grausam zu brechen dieses treuste Herz!
Dein Vater—ha! den Bräut'gam bracht'
er mit . . .
Wohl kenn' ich ihn . . . mir ahnte, was
geschieht!
Doch du . . . ist's möglich! — reichest
deine Hand
dem Mann, der deine Schwelle kaum
betrat!

SENTA
Nicht weiter! Schweig! Ich muss, ich
muss!

ERIK
O, des Gehorsams, blind wie deine Tat!
Den Wink des Vaters nanntest du will-
kommen,
mit *einem* Stoss vernichtest du mein
Herz!

SENTA
Nicht mehr! Nicht mehr! Ich darf dich
nicht mehr sehn,
nicht an dich denken: hohe Pflicht
gebeut's.

ERIK
Welch hohe Pflicht? Ist's *höh're* nicht,
zu halten,
was du mir einst gelobtest, ewige Treue?

SENTA
Wie? Ew'ge Treue hätt' ich dir gelobt?

ERIK
Senta, o Senta, leugnest du?
Willst jenes Tags du nicht dich mehr
entsinnen,
als du zu dir mich riefest in das Tal?
Als, dir des Hochlands Blume zu gewinnen,
mutvoll ich trug Beschwerden ohne
Zahl?

Hussassahey!
Reefs and storms, bah!

(*The sea, elsewhere calm, begins to rise in the neighborhood of the Dutch ship. A dark-bluish flame flares up like a watch-fire on the ship. A loud stormwind whistles through the cordage; the crew, hitherto invisible, rouse themselves up at the appearance of the flame.*)

DUTCHMAN'S CREW

Yohohe! Yohohohoey! hohohohoey!
  Hoey! Hoey! Hoey!
Huissa!
To the land drives the storm.
Huissa!
Furl the sails! Anchor free!
Hurry in to the bay!
Dusky captain, go ashore.
Seven years have passed away!
Woo a pretty maid and score!
Pretty maiden, love him well!
Merrily, hui!
Bridegroom, hui!
Stormwind howls bride-music,
Ocean has joined the dance!
Hui, hark, he pipes!
Really, captain, have you come back?
Hui, furl the sails!
And your bride, say, where is she?
Hui, off to sea!
Once again, once again, you've no
  luck in your love!
Ha, ha, ha!
Blow, O stormwind, howl away,
Sails like ours you'll never fray!
Satan has applied his art,
They will never tear apart.

(*During the song of the Dutchmen, their ship is tossed up and down by the waves. A frightful wind howls through the cordage. But all around the air and sea remain calm.*)

NORWEGIAN SAILORS

What a song! Are they spooks? How I
  fear!
Give your voice! Sing aloud!
Steersman, leave the watch, etc.

(*The Norwegian sailors, silenced by the storm, quit the deck, overcome with horror, and make the sign of the cross. The Dutchman's crew laughs. Immediately there is a calm, as before. Senta comes with trembling steps out of the house; Eric follows her, in agitation.*)

ERIC

What am I hearing? God! What must
  I see?
Illusion? Falsehood or the truth?

SENTA

Oh, do not ask! Do not expect me to
answer.

ERIC

O righteous God! No doubt then, it is
  true!
What most unblessed power swept you
  along?
What power prevailed on you so soon,
  cruelly to tear in two this faithful
  heart?
Your father? Ha, your father brought
  the groom.
Him I know well. The thing I
  feared has come!
But you—how could you! Reaching
  forth your hand
To one who crossed your threshold only
  now!

SENTA

No further! Stop! I must! I must!

ERIC

Oh, this obedience, blind as is your act!
Your father beckons and you gladly
  follow.
A single blow from you destroys my
  heart!

SENTA

No more! No more! I dare not see you
  more!
I must forget you, when high duty
  calls.

ERIC

What duty calls? What duty here is
  higher
Than that which made you pledge me
  love eternal?

SENTA

What? Love eternal? When was that
my pledge?

ERIC

Senta! O Senta! Why deny?
Is that a day you wish not to remember,
When from the vale you called me to
  your side,
When, just to win for you the highland flowers,
Fearless, unnumbered dangers I defied?

Gedenskt du, wie auf steilem Felsenriffe
vom Ufer wir den Vater scheiden sahn?
Er zog dahin auf weiss beschwingtem
  Schiffe
und meinem Schutz vertraute er dich
  an.
Als sich dein Arm um meinen Nacken
  schlang,
gestandest du mir Liebe nicht aufs neu?
Was bei der Hände Druck mich hehr
  durchdrang,
sag', war's nicht die Versichrung deiner
  Treu'?

(*Der Holländer hat den Auftritt be-
lauscht; in furchtbarer Aufregung
bricht er jetzt hervor.*)

HOLLÄNDER

Verloren! Ach, verloren!Ewig verlornes
Heil!

ERIK

Was seh' ich? Gott!

HOLLÄNDER

Senta, leb' wohl!

SENTA

(*sich ihm in den Weg werfend*)
Halt ein, Unsel'ger!

ERIK

Was beginnst du?

HOLLÄNDER

In See! In See—für ew'ge Zeiten!
Um deine Treue ist's getan,
um deine Treue—um mein Heil!
Leb' wohl, ich will dich nicht verderben!

ERIK

Entsetzlich! Dieser Blick . . . !

SENTA

Halt ein!
Von dannen sollst du nimmer fliehn!

HOLLÄNDER

(*gibt seiner Mannschaft ein gellendes
Zeichen auf einer Schiffspfeife*)

Segel auf! Anker los!
Sagt Lebewohl für Ewigkeit dem
  Lande!

SENTA

Ha! Zweifelst du an meiner Treue!
Unsel'ger, was verblendet dich?
Halt ein! Das Bündnis nicht bereue!
Was ich gelobte, halte ich!

ERIK

Was hör ich! Gott, was muss ich sehen!
Muss ich dem Ohr, dem Auge traun?
Senta! Willst du zugrunde gehen?
Zu mir! Du bist in Satans Klau'n!

HOLLÄNDER

Fort auf das Meer treibt's, mich aufs
  neue!
Ich zweifl' an dir, ich zweifl' an Gott!
Dahin! Dahin ist alle Treue!
Was du gelobtest, war dir Spott!
Erfahre das Geschick, vor dem ich dich
  bewahr'!
Verdammt bin ich zum grässlichsten
  der Lose:
Zehnfacher Tod wär' mir erwünschte
  Lust!
Vom Fluch ein Weib allein kann mich
  erlösen,
ein Weib, das Treu' bis in den Tod mir
  hält.
Wohl hast du Treue mir gelobt, doch
  vor
dem Ewigen noch nicht: dies rettet
  dich!
Denn wiss', Unsel'ge, welches das Ge-
  schick,
das jene trifft, die mir die Treue
  brechen:
Ew'ge Verdammnis ist ihr Los!
Zahllose Opfer fielen diesem Spruch
durch mich! Du aber sollst gerettet sein.
Leb wohl! Fahr hin, mein Heil, in
  Ewigkeit!

ERIK

Zu Hilfe! Rettet! Rettet sie!

SENTA

(*den Holländer aufhaltend*)

Wohl kenn' ich dich! Wohl kenn' ich
  dein Geschick!
Ich kannte dich, als ich zuerst dich sah!
Das Ende deiner Qual ist da! Ich bin's,
durch deren Treu' dein Heil du finden
  sollst!

Remember how from the steep and
  rocky mainland
We stood and watched your father sail
  away?
Do you recall, when white-winged vessel took him,
He to my care had trusted you that
  day?
Then, when your arm was twined
  around my neck,
Did you not own your love for me
  anew?
Why was I thrilled at pressure of your
  hand?
Say, was it not the assurance you were
  true?

(*The Dutchman has entered unper-
ceived and has been listening. He
comes forward in the greatest agitation.*)

DUTCHMAN

I'm done for! Lost forever! Lost
  through eternity!

ERIC

What is this? God!

DUTCHMAN

Senta! Farewell!

SENTA

(*turning toward him as he leaves*)
Oh stay! Poor wanderer!

ERIC

What possesses you?

DUTCHMAN

To sea, to sea!
To sail for endless ages!
Your faith and honor are no more,
Your faith and honor, and my cure!
Farewell! I wish not to destroy you!

ERIC

Oh horror! Oh that look!

SENTA

Oh stop! You'll never have to flee from
  hence!

DUTCHMAN

(*gives a loud signal on his pipe and
  calls to his crew*)

Set the sails! Anchor up! Then say a
  fond farewell to land forever!

SENTA

Ha, can you doubt that I am faithful?
Poor wanderer, what has blinded you?
Oh wait! Oh wait! Oh wait!
Do not repent your compact,
What I have promised shall I hold.
Oh wait! Stay here!

ERIC

What hear I? God, what am I seeing?
What should my ears, what should my
  eyes believe?
What hear I? God, Senta!
Are you resolved on ruin?
Come here! Come here! You are in
  Satan's clutch!

DUTCHMAN

Once more the sea urges me onward,
I doubt your word, I doubt my God!
Away, away with all truth and honor!
What you have promised was a jest!
Now learn about the fate
From which I've saved your soul:
The lot that I am doomed to bear is
  frightful.
Death would be ten times more a
  yearned-for bliss.
My curse is conquered only through a
  woman,
A woman who will keep her faith till
  death.
You, it is true, have sworn your truth,
Although not yet before your God: so
  you are saved!
For know, unhappy woman, of the fate
That comes to her who breaks the vow
  she makes me.
Endless damnation is her lot!
Victims untold have fallen beneath this
  curse through me.
You, truly, nonetheless are saved!
Farewell! Depart, my cure, for ever-
  more!

ERIC

Oh help her, save her, save her soul!

SENTA

(*stopping the Dutchman*)

Well do I know you, well do I know
  your fate.
I knew you too that time I saw you
  first.
Your time of torment now is done.
I am she through whose faith salvation
  shall be yours.

(*Auf Eriks Hilferuf sind Daland, Mary und die Mädchen aus dem Hause, die Matrosen von dem Schiffe herbeigeeilt.*)

ERIK

Helft ihr! Sie ist verloren!

DALAND, MARY UND CHOR

Was erblick' ich!

DALAND

Gott!

HOLLÄNDER

Du kennst mich nicht, du ahnst nicht, wer ich bin!
Befrag die Meere aller Zonen, befrag
den Seemann, der den Ozean durchstrich,
er kennt dies Schiff, das Schrecken aller Frommen:
den *fliegenden Holländer* nennt man mich!

(*Mit Blitzesschnelle langt er am Bord seines Schiffes an, das augenblicklich unter dem Seerufe der Mannschaft abfährt. Senta sucht sich mit Gewalt von Daland und Erik, die sie halten, loszuwinden.*)

MANNSCHAFT DES HOLLÄNDERS

Johohe! Johohoe! Hoe! Huissa!

DALAND, ERIK, MARY UND CHOR

Senta! Senta! Was willst du tun?

SENTA

(*hat sich mit wütender Macht losgerissen und erreicht ein vorstehendes Felsenriff. Von da aus ruft sie mit aller Gewalt dem absegelnden Holländer nach.*)

Preis deinen Engel und sein Gebot!
Hier steh' ich treu dir bis zum Tod!

(*Sie stürzt sich in das Meer; in demselben Augenblick versinkt das Schiff des Holländers und verschwindet schnell in Trümmern. Das Meer schwillt hoch auf und sinkt in einem Wirbel wieder zurück. In weiter Ferne entsteigen dem Wasser der Holländer und Senta, beide in verklärter Gestalt; er hält sie umschlungen.*)

ENDE DER OPER

ERIC

(*at whose cry for help Daland, Mary, and the maidens hasten from the house and the sailors from the ship*)

Help her, or she will perish!

DALAND, MARY AND CHORUS

What is happening?

DALAND

God!

DUTCHMAN

You know me not, suspect not who I am.
But ask the seas of every region,
Or ask the seaman who traverses ocean's realm;
He knows this ship, the terror of the pious:
The *Flying Dutchman* I am called!

(*The Dutchman boards his ship with quick stride. At once the ship leaves the shore and puts to sea. Senta wishes to hasten after the Dutchman, but her father, Mary and Eric hold her back.*)

DUTCHMAN'S CREW

Yo ho hoey!

MARY, ERIC, DALAND AND CHORUS

Senta, Senta, what will you do?

SENTA

(*who has freed herself violently and now ascends a cliff, overhanging the sea, from which she calls after the departing Dutchman with all her power*)

Praise to your angel and his decree!
Here stand I, faithful until death!

(*She casts herself into the sea. The Dutchman's ship, with all her crew, sinks immediately. The sea rises high, and sinks back in a whirlpool. In the glow of the sunset are clearly seen, over the wreck of the ship, the forms of Senta and the Dutchman, embracing each other, rising from the sea, and floating upward.*)

END OF THE OPERA